The MUTANT MALE

By

L.J. Gora

This book is dedicated to everyone who knows the future is not guaranteed and chooses to make a difference so that there will be a future.

How you think is how you speak.
How you speak is how you act.
How you act is who you are.

Table of Contents

Chapters

The Mutant Male

1. YOU BEGAN LIFE AS A FEMALE (EVEN IF YOU ARE A MALE)

All mammalian species, (that includes us, the human species), begin life as female and continues as female during the first six weeks of existence. The fertilized egg (or zygote) undergoes essentially a biochemical mutation to become a male. Thus, males are technically mutants of the primary gender which is female. Sorry guys.

Just to clarify, the definition of Mutant/Mutation is as follows: "A mutant or mutation is an organism or new genetic character arising from a change of the DNA sequence of a gene or chromosome. The occurrence of genetic mutations is basic to the process of adaptation a species must undergo to survive in a world of ever occurring changes."

2. IT IS ALL ABOUT BIOLOGY

Like it or not, you are your biology.   Now, all life strives to assure and continue the existence of itself. If this fails, you have extinction. From what we know, all life starts with proteins or large biomolecules which eventually evolve into combinations we refer to as genes.

These genes combine in precise ways to make up chromosomes. Chromosomes are basically a vast array of biochemical formulas for making specific physical and functional characteristics. These eventually form a new living organism.

Each species has a specific number of chromosomes. Humans, have a total of 46. This total is made up of 23 chromosomes from the mother's egg and 23 chromosomes from the father's sperm. In most cases, one sperm is allowed to enter one egg and this results in fertilization.

Fertilizing basically means the two sets of parental chromosomes have combined. This sets off a sort of chain reaction to form a template or master plan we call, DNA (Deoxyribonucleic acid). It shows up as a spiral structure that houses all the 46 chromosomes necessary to make a unique individual. This is what makes you, you.

Think about the incredible fact that a highly select series of biochemical interactions took place to make you who you are.

By the way, we are not from apes. All simians (apes, chimps, monkeys, orangutans, etc.), have 48 chromosomes, not 46, so not related. We came from similar ancient beginnings, but we are not an off-shoot of the simian. We can share similar "patterning", such as the genetic body design that makes the color brown for eyes or the bone and muscle patterns needed to create an opposable thumb, but you are not a monkey's uncle.

Another interesting side note is that your DNA isn't perfect. It has lots of broken bits and "garbage" structures in it. These bits generally get moved to the ends of the chromosomal structure. It is a little like shoving them out of the way. Humans have upwards of 200 of these "anomalies". Many of them cause life-threatening conditions, referred to as "genetic diseases". Oddly, other species have only about 20 of these anomalies in their gene sets and most are not considered life-threatening. They might show up as albinism, an extra toe or lack of a tail in an animal. A curious fact, don't you think?

3. YOU LEARNED TO MULTIPY AT A VERY EARLY STAGE

Now once these biochemical mechanisms are activated, they trigger workings within the cell causing it to reproduce itself. So, one cell becomes two cells, (they call them sister cells) and these sisters "split" again and become four and so on until there is this flat little blob of cells. This is the fertilized egg or zygote moving into an embryonic stage of development.

The blob of cells or embryo starts working as a cluster of like-minded cells that reproduce themselves to a point where the embryo can start developing all the (potentially) successful pattern combinations provided by both egg and sperm. This is the first step towards forming a successful new organism or person. *Everything about you is described in these patterns.* This stage goes on for about six weeks. The DNA combinations are incubating during this time and the incubation takes place in your mother's biological laboratory known as her uterus. The control center for this laboratory is your mother's brain.

The DNA isn't just about your eye or hair color, it contains every specific detail of your body. It identifies that your shape, form, and function will be human and not hummingbird. This activity is not restricted to just the stages of fetal body development, either. All the instructions for your body's growth, development and tendencies are present as well. The magnitude of information and instructions to process this genetic information would crash a super computer, maybe several super computers.

These embryonic cells carry within them everything needed to make you, such as the number of hair follicles on your head or the thickness of your stomach lining and even your tendency to like strawberry ice cream. You are your

DNA. If any part of a gene pattern is missing, incomplete or damaged in the DNA makeup, it shows up as a defect. This can be a visible or physical defect, however, it can also be a functional defect, like the inability to digest certain foods or repair broken bones. The quality of your DNA is important to your successful survival. So, pick your parents wisely.

The embryo is a stage of life with no body definition, organs or systems. It is essentially very smart cells with a plan to reproduce themselves. The cells with human DNA are not yet a person. That happens in the third trimester when the body identification by the fully formed brain takes place.

Think of this incubation period as the phase when the DNA combinations work out their patterns and lay out the shape of the body and organs. At this point the identity of female or male is only possible at the DNA level, because the structures that become sex organs don't exist. So, the gender identity of the developing organism is only relatable to its genetic base.

Since the primary base of the organism started as an egg, then a fertilized egg (zygote), the only gene present during this time is the 'X' gene. The "X" gene is female. So, for roughly six weeks during every human embryo's development, everyone is *female*. By the way guys, that's why you have non-functioning nipples. A remnant of the days when you were extremely young and female.

Now, science is still dominated mostly by males, who, I suspect, would rather ignore this little fact. Most (male) scientists prefer to refer to this period as a sexually indifferent period. They base their argument on the fact that sex organs don't exist at this stage. But let us revisit the definition of mutant - "A mutant is an organism or new genetic character arising from a change of the DNA

<u>sequence of a gene or chromosome</u>." That definition clearly describes the method that creates a male. Just to be clear, we all started, genetically, as females and males emerged because of genetic changes. The female gender is the primary gender. And, the male gender is the mutation.

4. WHY ARE THERE MUTANT MALES?

So, a good question would be how and why did males happen into existence. Well, we know the how. After the sixth week the embryo goes from looking like a flat blob to looking like a larvae or caterpillar-like form. In this three-dimensional stage the physical organs begin to take shape. Gonads (sex organs) start to develop and along with them are ducts that help produce sex hormones. Whether the offspring becomes male or remains female is influenced by gene combinations identified as "sex chromosomes". Visually, they look like the shape of a 'X' for female and 'Y' for male.

These sex chromosomes pair up with the original female gene. Structurally, it looks like 'XX' for female and 'XY for male. If the embryo's cells contain the 'XY' chromosome, it will also have an extra something called a **SRY gene**, which stands for <u>S</u>ex-determining <u>R</u>egion of the 'Y' chromosome. The *SRY* contains a protein that activates a gene network (think of it as manual of biochemical instructions) that tells the emerging non-specific sex organs (gonads) to start forming testes or what we call the male sex organs. If the Y chromosome and SRY are not present, then the gonads go their merry way and develop female sex organs or ovaries.

The beginning of sexual organ development is around the second month of pregnancy. Organs, themselves, are not fully present until around the twelfth week, and they are still not fully working organs. In a manner of speaking, they are the groundwork, like a 3-D blueprint which gets developed later in the fetal stage.

5. 'Y' DOES NOT EQUAL 'X' (FOR CAPACITY)

Now, picture the 'XX' and 'XY' shapes as storage cabinets for the protein codes (genes). The 'XX' has all the necessary storage space and information for both female and to some extent, male 'potential' development. The 'Y' storage cabinet by its very shape is missing storage space or the fourth leg of the 'X'. To offset and compensate for missing 'X' information, the SRY evolved as a specialized protein and catalyst, within the 'Y' gene. It activates the mutation process, and because the original genetic base was female, also carries bioagents that suppress female development. This way the SPY modifies the female's genetic foundation into a male's.

Another thing to consider is that more than gender specific, genetic information can be missing in the 'Y'. Remember, DNA has a lot of extra "garbage" in it with those 200 anomalies. Some of these can find their way into active sites, preventing better genes from getting a foot hold. This is how genetic malformations might occur.

Think of it this way, imagine you are packing to move. Some of you are very organized, putting everything correctly in the right place and using the packing space to its optimal level. Most DNA reflects this organizational method. But, some of you are terrible at packing and do a really bad job. You throw whatever you can into the boxes without caring if it fits and waste valuable space. You may even pack useless stuff or garbage. Well, sometimes DNA acts like this, too.

With the loss of genetic storage space on the 'Y', a greater chance of losing beneficial genes may occur because of "bad packing". Genes that aren't optimal or useful may take up key places on the DNA. Possible causes for this are covered later in the section about sperm. The male mutation is a sort of Russian roulette of genetics that biology gambles on for a winning outcome. Based on how our species has done, so far, biology would be considered a high-roller in Las Vegas. Anyway, this explains the 'how', but what about the 'why'?

6. WHY, OH WHY, OH WHY?

Consider a curious biological fact. A baby girl is born with approximately two million eggs nestled in her ovaries. This is her lifetime supply. Her health during fetal development and at the time of her birth, is reflected in her eggs. This includes the condition and health of her mother along with environmental influences during the nine-month pregnancy period. It isn't just about parental DNA. Now, not all the two million eggs are perfect, genetically or functionally speaking. But, statistically, with two million options the chances of getting a "good egg" are pretty high.

Males, on the other hand, produce sperm daily. The mutation that formed males puts them under a lot of pressure. Therefore, males need to ejaculate quite often. This pressure buildup is a reaction to the biological need to get out the old, and let in the new, so to speak. Take into consideration that the average male will produce roughly 525 billion sperm cells over a lifetime and shed at least one billion of them per month. It is estimated that a healthy adult male can release between forty million and 1.2 billion sperm cells in a single ejaculation. That's quite a lot. Aside from the question, "Who sat down and counted all these?", one could ask the question, "Why are sperm created daily, anyway?"

One reason is that human sperm cells are particularly vulnerable to free radical attack which can result in oxidative DNA damage. Sperm are also responsive to basic environmental changes such as food and water shortages, weather conditions, pollution, etc. The adaptivity of any species is possible through the genetic alterations contributed by the sperm. And as happens in nature, some adaptations work and others don't. If you are reading this book, your ancestors were successful in their adaptation. If you aren't reading this book because you don't exist, they failed.

The number and kind of changes that occurred to our human species isn't really known. We can make assumptions based on obvious physical differences. But let's take an example less know, that certain early humans couldn't see the color blue. Think of it as an early color blindness which most humans have overcome.

Blue has a very narrow wave-length which represents a very high frequency. The eye had to evolve specialized cones to "see" it. The broadest wave-length (or lowest frequency) we can see is the color red. Seeing red was necessary for survival because many foods are reddish, blood is red, etc. Blue was not a priority color because there are no blue foods or blue threats. Two colors humans still can't see are ultraviolet and infrared. Thanks to a mutation, blue started to register on the back of the human eye and in the human brain as a color.

Once discovered, the ancient Egyptians loved blue. The Mediterranean populations, however, loved red. It seems that even as late as 850 BC, many of them may have had trouble seeing blue. This theory comes from a comment by the ancient Greek poet, Homer, where he describes the Mediterranean Sea as a dark maroon color, like the color of wine. Well, anyone who has seen the Mediterranean Sea, either in person or pictures, would say it is a very deep blue.

Another interesting contrast of ancient Egyptian and ancient Mediterranean cultures is that the formal legal status of Egyptian women (whether unmarried, married, divorced or widowed) was nearly identical with that of Egyptian men. Greek and Roman cultures, however, did not regard women as equal to men before the law. Did evolving to see the color blue have an influence on social behavior? Blue is routinely referred to as calming, while red excites. The expression, "seeing red" is often used for feeling angry. This leads to the interesting Siberian Fox Experiment.

7. FLOPPY EARED FOXES

Dmitri K. Belyaev, a Russian scientist, has been credited with being most responsible for our understanding of the domestication of canines, that is, how wild wolves turned into tame dogs. That was the original point to his research in 1948. But the outcomes showed that the anatomical and physiological changes, such as seen in domesticated dogs, could have been the result of breeding for behavioral traits. More specifically, he believed that tameness was the critical factor in changing how a dog looked.

In his breeding experiment, as the foxes became tamer, their physical appearance changed. Foxes' normal red coats changed dramatically in color and developed patterns. The fur color became white, gray or brown. Patterns showed up like dark spots (similar to Dalmatians) or multicolored bridling (like Beagles). Curly hair showed up, as did floppy ears. Just to clarify, there are no floppy ears in wild predators, it isn't a good ear shape for hearing well.

Genetics was in its infancy in 1948, so this research was done through selective breeding and then post-mortem physical examination of the animals. The first change Belyaev noticed was in the pituitary-adrenal axis. This system is responsible for the control of adrenaline, (among other things). The adrenaline hormone is one that produces a response to stress and controls most fear-related responses. There were significantly lower adrenaline levels in the experimental foxes than the control-group. His hypothesis was that since the foxes were less afraid of humans their bodies produced less adrenaline when around humans. This explained the foxes' tameness, but it didn't explain the changes in fur color and patterns or the floppy ears. The final theory concluded that adrenaline shares a biochemical pathway with melanin, which controls pigment production in fur. About now, you might be thinking, yes, interesting, but what does this have to do with mutant males?

Well, this experiment is described for two reasons. First, Belyaev did his genetic manipulation the old-fashioned way, through selective breeding. The breeding process allowed the fox's full component of DNA material to create the modifications to the body. And, because nature was allowed to do the modifications, Belyaev discovered the complex interdependency of temperament to glandular hormone production, resulting in physical modifications. It is a very holistic (dare I say female) viewpoint. Bodies, even those of foxes, are complex, interdependent systems, and this complexity is often overlooked by male thinking.

Instead, genetic research thinking is linear and compartmentalized. Scientists isolate genes, which is good for identification purposes. But, they manipulate singular genes focused on obtaining a singular outcome in a biological system that is interconnected and very complex. Well, this approach is a little like playing Jenga™ blindfolded. You don't know what is dependent on what and when a gene is removed or altered, the result may topple the whole structure. Dinking with the DNA of any organism, whether plant or animal, through the isolated gene approach can trigger unforeseen consequences. But this (male) thinking method predominates most genetic research and science, in general.

Secondly, the outcome of the research hints at interconnected mechanisms that result in behavior and physical modifications. Are behavioral differences within a species, including humans, the catalysts for physical changes within that species? Belyaev couldn't further his research at a genetic level because the technology wasn't available. But it raises the old question of what is a stronger influence, nature or nurture. Given the research results, the question is wrong. These aspects aren't in competition (male thinking, again), they collaborate (female trait).

Humans like to think of themselves as special, apart from animals. Nope, you are a fully paid member of the animal kingdom. So, it is possible that the diversity of the human race cannot be just a factor of environmental challenges but a result of behavioral changes as well.

8. YOU HAVE NOTHING TO FEAR, BUT FEAR ITSELF (Franklin Delano Roosevelt)

The emotion of fear is a core component of all life. It is a survival mechanism and generates a response to danger, "flight or fight". Fear is a combination of brain activity, hormonal release, specifically adrenaline and a physical response. But, fear is also a learned response. The fox research showed that as conditions become less threatening, the brain/body connection manifested physical changes, thus DNA changes. Might this also account for spontaneous changes in human skin color, eye color and hair color? What about seeing the color blue? Could this also account for skeletal modifications, such as changes in the shape of the cranium or bone lengths?

Assumptions made about our ancestors' appearance are that they looked like apes. This is a hold-over from Darwinism, due to how we resemble them with similar body structures. However, we had from fifteen to twenty humanoid ancestors as far as we know. What if our more docile humanoid ancestors looked different? Some of their traits could have managed their way into our gene pool. As a comparison, let's take Orangutans, for instance, who are extremely gentle, intelligent apes. They have red hair. Chimps, on the other hand can be nasty and even violent (apologies to Jane Goodall). They tend to be smallish, brownish and churlish. Gorillas are intelligent, shy and gentle, unless threatened. Koko, the gorilla even learned sign language. They are large with silver gray to almost black colored hair. Basically, all these simians have different behavior and they all have different body types and coloring from one another.

We can't selectively breed humans to test this theory, although we might get volunteers, if we asked nicely. But, we know that specific races with defined physical traits are found clustered in specific geographical locations. Geography is an environmental catalyst for human behavior. Human beings behave differently in different climates. Human behaviors resulting in physical traits may be partially due to how harsh or benign conditions were for the humans living in those regions.

Societies and eventually cultures, are based on common behavioral traits, too. Warm, lush or tropical locations tend to create easy going lifestyles whereas harsher, colder locals seem to foster tribal attitudes that often support less friendly and more aggressive societies, especially towards outsiders.

Living under harsher conditions would trigger fear hormones more frequently. Long-term effects from these powerful biochemical hormones could result in permanent glandular and possibly brain function changes. Eventually a population might develop physical characteristics that favored specific behavior patterns. The diversity of physical appearances which we call race, may be a result of how each group behaved and the resulting evolution based, in part, on their behavior.

This wouldn't be a one-way street, however. Life is a cyclic process. Behavior modifies body chemistry which creates genetic alterations which modifies appearance which alters behavior, that environmental conditions again modify, which again changes body chemistry and so on. Let's just say, it is an interesting question to consider. Does behavioral change over time, influenced by environment, cause the emergence of physical differences in humans, as it did in foxes?

9. YOU ALONE, ARE NOT A CLONE

Nature went to a lot of trouble and risk for the female to produce a male. How come? Well, we know that higher mammals do not reproduce through cloning. Yes, clones have been created in laboratories, but in-depth studies of the cloned outcomes show that cloned organisms experience weakened DNA patterning. Think of a photocopy of a letter as an example. The more it is reproduced the less defined and crisp the print. Higher life forms have complexities in their DNA structures that undergo stress when cloned, it wears out the original pattern. Also, repeatedly using the same DNA, over, and over again, does not improve the gene pool. Cloning isn't practical for humans. The male gender is designed to provide genetic diversity, the introduction of new genetic material into any given group of females, thus into the species. This is just the simple version. Life is a multidimensional, complexity of continuous formation, destruction and reformation. By the way, since nature does not condone cloning, it begs the question, "Why are we wasting resources by trying to do it?" More mutant male thinking?

10.   KNOW YOUR SPERM, KNOW YOURSELF

This part is all about your little guys, guys. It may be more interesting to males reading this book, but females are invited to read it too. As mentioned, your sperm's chromosomes are vulnerable to environmental factors. This suggests that males play a big role in the genetic mechanism that adapts or evolves the species to environmental conditions. Damage to the sperm may also result in genetic malformations. Overall, males seem to be kind of a mixed blessing. Ask any female.

If you are a male, think about how much you know about your sperm. Since it is the primary reason for your existence, you should have at least more than a passing interest in these wiggly little reproductive cells you produce daily in great numbers. In fact, sperm production may be your only biological purpose for existing. So, here goes.

The human sperm cell consists of a head, neck, a midpiece and a tail. Basically, it looks and moves like a tadpole. The head has a central part called the nucleus, that houses the DNA. Surrounding the head of the sperm is something called an acrosome. Think of it as a chemical football helmet on the head of your sperm. It contains enzymes that help the sperm to penetrate the wall of the female egg. But, it also contains other important enzymes that help the sperm's membranes to fuse with the egg's membranes, otherwise they can't make connections to share DNA.

The next part of the sperm is the neck, a section between the head and tail. It contains a tubular structure called a centriole. The centriole is another extremely important part of your sperm. It is the part that triggers the fertilization process. If this part is damaged, then it is infertile. Keep in mind that all these parts are vulnerable to damage, either through health issues or environmental toxins. So, infertility isn't just a numbers game.

Included within the centriole are structures called centrosomes. These little guys are responsible for helping the new cells that are forming keep their shape. Important because you don't want your baby looking like a melted marshmallow or Jabba the Hut, from the movie, "Star Wars".

Sperm are more than DNA carriers. Studies back in 1991 showed that the human embryo inherits the father's centrosome at fertilization through a single centriole. Interestingly, this centrosome takes over and becomes active while the mother's centrosome is reduced and becomes inactive. This is because only one centrosome can be functioning in normal development. In a nutshell, healthy father and healthy sperm equals healthy baby development

The midpiece of the sperm has a central core that looks like a lot of fibers and around these are little powerhouse cells called mitochondria. Think of these as little motors or engines. They use a high energy molecule called ATP (Adenosine triphosphate) to produce the energy for the tail or "flagellum" to make its lashing movements. This is how the tail propels the sperm forward, much like the motion of a tadpole.

There you are, fellows, all about the sperm that defines you. And, you thought it was all about your penis. Wrong! The penis is just a dispenser for shooting out the real important bits, your sperm. These little DNA carriers are tough. They can live inside a female for up to 5 days. A lot of your gender traits show up in your Mini-Me's too. Male traits, such as being aggressively competitive, for example, are shown in their actions as they push their way up stream (or downstream?) to get to their goal. And, like all males, they are linearly focused on one goal. To keep the species going.

But these little guys face an onslaught of deadly conditions in today's world which they have never faced before. And, this has been brought about by their very creators, mutant males.

11. TWITCH YOUR NOSE, WIGGLE YOUR EARS, SHAKE YOUR TAIL, YOU'RE A LAB RAT

Recent research on mice shows that after the initial formation of sperm cells, the cells are very sensitive to environmental genotoxic agents. This means that as the sperm cells develop to maturity, they start to lose the ability to repair DNA damage if genotoxins are present.

Other research (on mice) shows that damaged sperm can cause damage to the DNA of the mother's egg as well. It can cause it to break down or fail to connect strands creating what looks like sores in the matrix of the egg.

Unfortunately, our world is saturated with genotoxic agents. They are in our workplaces, in our water, food, air, in the fabric of our clothing and in almost all products and items we use daily. In addition, the introduction of genetically modified foods (GMO's) is altering food sources at basic levels. GMO's were only introduced in 1994. There has been no time to fully assess possible long-term effects on human health or the human gene pool. And, remember the foxes. Changes to any living thing has consequences.

Basically, the existing human population, (you and me) can consider itself and its off-springs in the role of laboratory rats. We are unwitting participants in a great uncontrolled experiment that is altering the future condition of human beings, as well as other species. And, you can bet not in a good way. So, twitch your nose, wiggle your ears, shake your tail, you're a lab rat.

Still in doubt? It is estimated that an roughly **eighty to two hundred toxic chemicals are in your body right now**. *Everybody's blood contains toxic chemicals, worldwide.* These toxins are very democratic. You have them whether rich or poor, powerful or meek. You cannot escape having these chemicals in your blood. And, you cannot get rid of them or escape exposure to them. They are everywhere and in almost everything. Scientists have defined a new term for this condition. It is called the "toxic body burden". Not just humans but all species on the planet are dealing with toxic body burdens. The extent of self-imposed contamination has never been experienced before in the history of the planet, by the way.

This level of pollution really took off around the end of World War II. That's when the petrochemical corporations, who benefited greatly from the war, now had to face a loss of profits in peace time. Ah, shucks, how to keep making money now that peace broke out. To keep their wealth, they focused on producing plastics, fertilizers, pesticides, drugs, and the vast array of products we take for granted today.

Unfortunately, these were all produced synthetically through petroleum processing and chemical methods that weren't/aren't regulated for safety, created environmental pollutants and whose extraction caused non-reversible environmental damage.

But, they produce stuff people love, like plastics. In fact, humans produce two hundred, sixty million tons of plastic each year, worldwide. About 10% of this plastic ends up in the oceans as trash. The amount of plastic garbage is so enormous that a plastic island-like mass the size of the state of Rhode Island is growing in the Pacific Ocean.

Plastic, like radiation, takes thousands of years to decay. It breaks down eventually into micro-particles that are consumed by fish and wildlife. Numerous species of marine life now deal with increasing toxic body burdens. Consequently, their toxic bodies enter the human food chain. Yes, waiter, I would like the grilled plastic with a side of heavy metals and a glass of chemical waste product. Yummy.

If you were born in the late 1970's, you already have a lifelong accumulation of toxic chemical exposure. Anywhere from eighty to over two hundred toxins are floating in your blood stream as you read this sentence. What does this mean to your health? We don't know. But the production of these toxic products is very good for business. The mutant males who are CEO's of corporations say it strengthens the economy. These guys complain that government oversight and regulation are bad. They support unfettered production without accountability and claim it makes business stronger, and the human race weaker. But that is why drug companies were created, right? To put us out of our misery with more chemicals in the form of drugs.

In 2005 the Environmental Working Group (EWG) did a research investigation and found that over two hundred toxic compounds, collectively, were in the cord blood of ten newborn infants. Chilling thought considering they still have their whole life ahead of them.

12.   THE LEGACY OF LITTLE BOY AND FAT MAN

Did I mention that radiation levels worldwide are elevated too? Again, this has been since the end of WW II. Thanks to the push for profits by military industrial corporations (owned and operated by mutant males), the manufacturing of nuclear weapons and atomic bomb testing, nuclear power plant construction and associated radioactive waste are raising the radiation levels of the environment to an all-time high. Add to this the radiation released from nuclear accidents at Chernobyl and Fukushima, and erosion of the ozone which allows greater solar radiation exposure. The world described in the movie, "Mad Max, Fury Road", starts to look like a plausible future. By the way, mutant males love that movie.

Today's world is filled with mutant males in leadership positions who believe that bigger is better. They also have no problem using chemical weapons, imprisonment, torture, bombings, suppression of civil rights as the way of securing their male power. They use the threat of nuclear weapons to prove their mutant macho maleness. They even consider using nuclear weapons at the risk of annihilation, just to prove they are the "the big guy", "in control". They proclaim, as in the movie, "The Life of Brian", "I am Biggus Dickus." Please, someone, save us all from Male Vanity!

Unfortunately, these mutant males forget that strontium-90 and cesium-137 have half-lives of about thirty years (half the radioactivity will decay in thirty years). And, plutonium-239 has a half-life of twenty-four thousand years. Once in the atmosphere this stuff spreads worldwide through ocean and wind currents. Why do mutant males think they are exempt from the consequences of their actions? Maybe because we haven't held them accountable.

One large collection of mutant males is currently in the Republican controlled United States government (yes, I know mutant males are a worldwide scourge. But the U.S. has some of the best examples I could find.). So, using the U.S. example, the Republican (GOP) party has fought against providing its citizens with national health care. They also worked to remove regulations for both environmental and chemical safety standards. GOP leadership favors its corporate overlords over the country and its citizens.

Aside from their greed and graft, these mutant males realize it is not cost effective to poison your people and then pay out money to try and heal them. Republican mutant male legislators (okay, not all of them, but certainly the pack leaders) do not want to spend money on the healthcare of lab rats, sorry, citizens, because they see it as a lost cause. Besides, they get more kickbacks from strong corporations as compared to weak citizens.

But, the universe is an equal opportunity provider. Again, we should be reminded that although these politicians have voted themselves excellent healthcare coverage, they too are exposed to all the same toxins as everyone else. So, guess what GOP dudes, you are lab rats, too!

13. MALES MAY BE HAZARDOUS TO MOM'S HEALTH

That females can produce males at all shows the amazing adaptability of the human body. Remember, male's embryonic and fetal development takes place within the environment of a *female* body. The internal environment of a female's body is hormonally balanced for successful support of the female and can develop the female offspring without extraordinary hormonal alteration.

This is not the case with support of a male embryo and fetus. The mother's body must produce an alternate internal condition related to male development and hormones. This means mom experiences an excess of testosterone (a primary male hormone), at levels not normal for her body. Her body experiences an onslaught of a variety of supportive male hormones along with moderate suppression of some of her female hormones. This places the mother's body in a constant state of fluctuating hormonal stress.

The dilemma is that she needs to keep her female hormones flowing to support her reproductive health and ability. But at the same time, she is dealing with higher than normal male hormone levels to develop the male body. This is one reason why many pregnant women experience severe hormonal fluctuations. Hormones are very powerful biochemicals. The presence, absence or any dramatic change in hormone levels affects both maternal and fetal health and can impact their bodies' ability to function.

The stress the female body experiences in trying to cope with oscillating female/male hormones results in emotional, mental and physical conditions that can be extremely painful and debilitating. The significance of this isn't fully appreciated. This is due, in part, to the historically skewed male perception of the unimportance of female issues, such as pregnancy. This is a basic attitude of most male dominated societies and cultures. Because males do not experience pregnancy they do not have the capability of comprehending its impact on the body. Lucky them.

Pregnancy is labeled a natural occurrence. This is even expressed by other females, again, a social or cultural bias. Yet, never assume there is safety in the term "natural". Infection, vomiting and diarrhea are natural events, as is decay and death. Most of you would not want to participate in these 'natural' actions. The true definition of natural is that it is something that happens in nature, not that it is safe.

Every pregnant female is biologically programmed to be a life giver to a fully complete and, hopefully, healthy human being. Since the process has been perfected over eons of biological evolution, it is taken for granted. Pregnancy is even minimalized as routine and a normal occurrence.

Yet currently, in the United States, which considers itself a world leader, the mortality rate for mothers is the highest of all the modern, industrialized countries in the world. In fact, mothers in the U.S. are more likely to die from the complications of pregnancy and childbirth now than they would have two decades ago. Death rates are in the double digits and rising. Sadly, this is not only true in the U.S. (at 14%) but also in Canada (at 11%). So, rates for these two 'modern' countries have gone up while a small drop of 2.3% in the death rate for mothers has happened worldwide.

Not surprisingly these two countries (and many others) have deeply entrenched patriarchal societies. There is a cultural façade which thinly hides an underbelly of misogyny. Political platitudes of equality, opportunity and freedom are declared while females are routinely harassed and attacked because of their gender. They are targets and sexual objects just because they are female. There are also high rates of violent crimes against females in these industrialized countries.

Furthermore, patriarchal cultures support fundamental religious dogmas which claim females are happiest when serving as domestic servants and breeding stock. These dogmas preach against the female having sovereignty over her own body. Pro-lifers claim the sanctity of life while practicing profanity against the female body. The hypocrisy was best summed up by the comedian, the late, George Carlin (one of my favorite and certainly evolved, mutant males). He remarked "Why are conservatives obsessed with the unborn, but once you're born, you're on your own. They don't want to know about you.". He also added, "If you are pre-born, you're fine." "If you are pre-school, you're f**ked" (rhymes with ducked). Another cryptic comment he said was, "How come when it is us, it's an abortion, but when it's a chicken, it's an omelet?"

Because mutant males see females as objects, they have no problem using the female body to sell merchandise. Popular media and advertising consistently displays unrealistic female body standards in movie roles, media or marketing strategies. The female image is made to fit the mutant male's desire of how a female body should look. This seems to be a body shaped like a skinny, teenaged boy with large breasts. The unrealistic appearance of bone thin, airbrushed models, results in young girls thinking of themselves as body failures, even though they are exactly as nature intended. This brainwashing has created body harming behavior in many females. Female eating disorders, cosmetic surgeries and self-mutilating behavior are on the rise. Sadly, self-harm has become a female trait.

14.   OUR CHILDREN, OUR FUTURE?

Here are some sobering statistics describing the female social situation of today in the U.S. Approximately 80% of the twelve million single-parent families in the United States, are headed by women. Approximately 60% of the children living in mother-only families are impoverished. That means that one out of five children live in poverty. The inclination of this society is to blame the mothers. But let us compare with another country that has a high single mother population.

Sweden has very high single mother rates. But, these single mother families have very low poverty rates. This is because Sweden's policies support caring for children in families. Sweden provides universal health care, generous paid parental and family leave, parenting education, child care (including high quality early childhood education) and other caring public policies.

Most of the U.S. females are the sole support for their children. Many of them work, one, two, even three jobs to make ends meet because wage discrepancy still exists. Promotional prejudice and gender-based jobs also keeps "women in their place", in the workplace.

This gender prejudice isn't fading out with the younger generation, either. Let me share the results of a recent impromptu survey done by a TV talk show host. He asked children, roughly twelve years old and under, "Why are women paid less than men?" Responses posted on YouTube (Kids Explain Why Women Are Paid Less Than Men, Jimmy Kimmel Live) were for seven little girls and four little boys.

These comments are from the little girls:

"(women) don't work as hard, they text and run on the track",

"They don't have jobs",

"They do stuff a little bit wrong, she don't know the stuff or the guy didn't teach her the stuff",

"They care about shopping more than work",

"They need equal rights",

"Because all the men make all the decisions and all of the rules", and

"The world is a messed-up place".

The four little boys responded:

"Because maybe they act weird",

"Men work harder",

"They are underrated and can do more, but people expect them to do less, but they can do so much more. They can do jobs men can't, like be an actress. They can do whatever their heart tells them to", and

"They are very good and work all the time, like my mom. (men) work too. My mom (works harder)."

Okay, got to love those last two little boys and their comments. But keep in mind that four of the seven little girls had serious prejudice against their own gender. How does this promote self-esteem in later life if little girls see their own gender from this negative perspective?

But gender bigotry is so pervasive that even the words, "girls" and "ladies", are routinely used as slights or slurs by males towards other males to imply weakness or failure. Guys in sports or the military often berate each other using comments like, "Stop being such a girl." or "Is this getting too tough for you, ladies?" Yet, the words "boys" or "gentlemen" are not used as insults among females. Most females would be confused if someone called them a "gentleman".

This might be a good time to introduce a bit of history. Why? Well, your thoughts, attitudes and behavior are more deeply rooted in the past than you think. There is a great saying, "The past causes the present, and so the future."

15.   ANCIENT MUTANT MALES TOLD LYING GENDER TALES

About now you might be thinking, so what? This history of gender bigotry against the female is well known and well documented. Isn't that how things are?

The point is that the suppressive and abusive treatment of women exists because of the opinions and writings of *mutant males*. As an example, the ancient Greek philosopher, Aristotle, saw woman, as an inferior sort of man. Could this be why the epitome of the female body, by today's male media standards, is a thin teenaged boy with big boobs? Males invented standards and values based on male attributes, such as strength, which females, generally, could not match. They measured intelligence through the training of logic, while females were denied education. Basically, they stacked the deck against the female. No surprise.

It stands to reason that the female's health and well-being play a significant role in the overall health and well-being of the human off-spring. What is often ignored or overlooked is how female health influences the health and strength of a country's population. This, in turn, impacts economic factors and cultural advancements of a nation.

I stress this because even today in the twenty-first century, patriarchal cultures still exist that allow females to be routinely harassed, bullied, mutilated and even murdered. This is based on the viewpoint that females have little value. This attitude is both insulting and outdated. In addition, mutant male ideology continues to emphasize dominance and violence as the go-to solutions for solving problems both domestically and internationally. The way males think today is both highly archaic and extremely dangerous not only for females, but for the world.

16.   THE CURIOUS STATE OF SPARTA

Speaking of archaic and dangerous, in ancient Greece there was the kingdom called Sparta. It was an incredible experiment that demonstrated two social extremes. On one hand it was a male dominated society based on, what I can only call, "testosterone toxic" military, mutant male machismo. And in extraordinary contrast, Sparta's females were allowed a level of liberty and freedom unknown to most women of the ancient Greek world. Go figure.

Modern movie audiences may be familiar with Sparta through the 2007 movie, "300", which depicted in true Hollywood fashion, a very buff and curiously animated Gerard Butler playing the Spartan King, Leonidas. The movie depicts the especially heroic stand of 300 Spartans at the critical Battle of Thermopylae in 480 B.C. They held off thousands of Persians for three days which gave the other Greek states time to pull together a defense. Thus, Sparta's action helped prevent the Persians from conquering the Greek states. Unfortunately, all 300 Spartans died.

Spartan culture was extremely harsh and deadly to its little boys. Imagine living in the very worst, most brutal boot camp, then multiply its intensity about 100 to 200 times. This is what the surviving Spartan boys were made to endure.

By surviving, I mean that Spartan baby boys (and girls) who weren't born healthy or fit were tossed off a cliff, to prevent the possibility of retrieval or survival. At around six-years or seven-years of age, boys were taken from their families and removed into the wilderness. They were under the "mentorship" of older men. These children were taught survival and military skills in the most brutal fashion. They had to hunt and kill their food, endure exposure to the elements and were encouraged to fight and even attack each other to stay alive. Because Sparta's entire culture centered on war, very extreme, macho behavior was considered the ideal.

Values drilled into every little surviving boy were of lifelong dedication to military discipline, service, and precision. Spartan vices were showing fear, the desire to want wealth or collect material stuff, and complaining or showing weakness. The ancient world was a brutal place and the Spartan culture molded these little boys into brutal little beings. These attributes gave the Spartan kingdom a strong advantage over other Greek civilizations, allowing it to dominate Greece in the fifth century B.C.

This extremely macho culture produced an ironic twist in its attitude towards women. Most ancient Greeks firmly believed that the male was the epitome of human perfection. We know this from the writings of their philosophers, such as Aristotle, Plato and Socrates. Females were considered basically imperfect. The woman was declared inferior and therefore subject to domination by the superior man.

An outcome of this belief was the idea that a man could only have a true relationship with another man, since it was impossible to have a true relationship with an inferior, i.e., a woman. Thus, homosexuality was considered normal and even expected in ancient Greek societies, as was pederasty (men having sex with little boys). Sparta's men interacted very little with women and when they did it was mostly to marry and breed children.

Despite this cultural attitude, the Spartan kings recognized an important fact which altered their approach to their women. They realized that to have healthy, strong baby boys (to grow into warriors for the Spartan army), the mothers had to be strong and healthy, too.

Women in the other Greek states, like Athens, lived very cloistered lives, much like women in some Middle Eastern cultures do today. They were veiled and restricted in their actions. In Sparta, however, girls and young women were expected to engage in outdoor sporting activities, including wrestling, javelin throwing and marathon running. Young girls and young boys even competed against each other in sporting events. Because of their healthy, active lifestyle, Spartan women were reported to be the most beautiful of Greek women. For example, the "face that launched a thousand ships", Helen of Troy, was originally Helen of Sparta.

Since the men lived in barracks, concentrated on military exercises and engaged in campaigns, they were never involved in domestic issues. They expected their women to be educated in handling these affairs. So, running the estates or farms, managing the slaves and overseeing domestic chores like planting, harvesting, taking care of the livestock, spinning, weaving, etc., was managed by the women. Thus, ironically, the very macho Spartan culture with its militaristic society provided a level of equality to its women that didn't exist in any other of the Greek states. For once, practicality and common sense won out over male vanity.

This shift in attitude emerged, as well, during both World War I and II. When there were too few employable males available, suddenly females were expected to fill the jobs of drivers, service workers, also work in aircraft and arms factories. Rosie, the riveter, rolled up her sleeves and got to work making battleships and bombers. Females were directly involved in support of military actions as nurses, ambulance drivers, couriers, and agents. Once the war was over, however, Rosie was expected to meekly go back to the kitchen.

I share this fun fact with you because it demonstrates a reality that patriarchal cultures tend to ignore. Strong, healthy women can do the same work as men, plus produce strong healthy babies.

17.   MUTANT MALES THINK IN STRAIGHT LINES

Now most humans don't greatly value their bodies or know how they work. That is, of course, until their bodies don't work. Males often take better care of their cars than they do of their bodies. So, on average, they tend to take a lot for granted when it comes to their body, the very thing they live in.

Perhaps the root of this disregard for the body is due to the fact that their body was free. No one values a freebie in the same way they appreciate something that requires a payment. Human (male?) opinion is that value is directly related to how much something costs. Yet, you can't buy health or a new body.

In addition, males don't consider that the very way they interpret the world is influenced by their biology and their gender. Here, I am referring to actual differences in the thought processes between the male and female brains.

For example, as hinted at before, male brains perceive the world in a linear way. This thought process causes them to create a world of hierarchies and categories, like class systems, with their associated dominance and submissive social positions. These systems require one person or select group to dominate, and the rest to be subservient.

Out of this idea was created the concept of titles. Titles announce or claim levels of importance, such as emperor, king, fuhrer, president, minister, khalif and husband. This satiates the needs of male vanity. But, inferior rankings must also exist, like slave, servant, peasant, serf, and wife. Otherwise the superior titles mean nothing. Of course, these hierarchies always include special economic, social and legal privileges to those at the top.

Another aspect of linear thinking is that any action is acceptable, if it gets you what you want. For example, violence is justified, ethics need not apply. This attitude is evident in sayings, such as, "the end justifies the means", "winner takes all, "last man standing wins", "to get what you want you have to take it", "greed is good" and "what's in it for me?"

Combine these behavioral concepts together with male vanity and it explains why most of *his*tory is a recounting of wars and conquests, brutality and violence, subjugation and control. The "end justifies the means" thinking describes the basic "A + B = C" male universe.

Of course, not all males think like this, many were more balanced in their thinking. But the dominant male culture forces compliance. If a more harmonious male does not fit in, he may be ostracized. Thus, mutant behavior and mutant influence has been imposed not only on the female half of the human species, but the whole species itself.

Female brains operate in a more holistic manner. This allows them to grasp a wide range of information and see the interconnectedness of things. Females can deal with multiple conditions, grasp their relationships and see the range of possible impacts. Females tend to favor cooperative efforts and support actions towards a common aim. Females tend to be socialists (politically and socially).

They prefer to share resources, protect the weak and work cooperatively. They developed as the original multi-taskers.

Think of it this way, male thinking is like using a fishing pole to fish for information. Female thinking is like casting a net to gather information. But males have been in control for so long, a sort of Stockholm syndrome has taken place in the female. The effect is a brainwashing that believes the male's way of thinking is the correct way of thinking. Male values, standards and opinions are considered the better ones. To reinforce these attitudes, males have historically categorized female thinking as ignorant, stupid or even crazy. Thanks, guys.

18.　　IT IS ALL ABOUT BALANCE

Are you angry about the negative description of males as toxic mutants? If you are female, you may feel the impulse to protect your males, whether father, husband, son, nephew, etc. You might claim your guys are the nicest specimen of maleness you know. Fair enough. Not all males are toxic, although they still are mutants. The nice guys aren't the problem. It's the other ones, the extremely toxic males, that are causing problems.

Males (and females) should strive to be fairly well-balanced human beings. It can be done when and if they operate within both their male and female aspects. This means males can be nurturing and supportive (female traits), as well as assertive (male characteristic) and do so when it is necessary and appropriate. Basically, any evolved human that respects others (the good ol' Golden Rule), whether male or female, is a balanced human being. Seeking a harmonious balance of male and female aspects is a good goal towards being an evolved human.

If you are not sure about gender behavior, here's a short list comparing gender traits. Some are a result of biology. Other traits are the viewpoints of societies.

Some Gender Assumptions for *MALES:*	*Some Gender Assumptions for* *FEMALES:*
Strong	Weak
Aggressive	Docile
Controlled	Hysterical
Dominant	Passive
Stoic	Emotional
Independent	Dependent
Intelligent	Silly
Focused	Scattered
Determined	Indecisive
Protective	Nurturing
Competitive	Collaborative

From these traits the definitions of man and woman have developed. I purposely use female and male throughout this book because it defines gender based on biology, which is more accurate than societal definitions. You are your biology, it can't be helped. 'Man' and 'woman' are inventions of society and culture. These labels are burdened with a lot of expected behaviors and restrictions, for both genders. Most characteristics of these gender roles are defined by extreme mutant male influences.

Don't think that females are off the hook for bad behavior. In fact, females can be as toxic and deadly, brutal and vicious as males. For example, the most prolific British serial killer was a female named Amelia Dyer. Not as famous as Jack the Ripper, but certainly as coldblooded and deadly. Her victims numbered around an estimated three to four hundred infants and young children over a thirty-year period. She ran a baby farm, taking in unwanted infants and children of single or poor women, under the pretense of finding them good homes. Most ended up at the bottom of the Thames River.

The opposite extreme of the testosterone toxic mutant male is an estrogen excessive female. Just as expected, this would be a female who was a passive-aggressive, whining, excessively verbal, self-proclaimed victim that lacked focus or direction. Basically, it would be someone you walk away from feeling drained of energy. In short, gender extreme individuals should be avoided at all times for safety and sanity.

BUT, (yes, notice the BIG BUT), males have not been the ones repressed, denied rights and even murdered for thousands of years. (Okay, males do kill each other, but they choose to do so.). It is important to point out the damaging influence of testosterone toxic macho, mutant male regimes on just about everything and everyone.

You may claim it is much better for females in today's society. After all, we have indoor plumbing, cell phones, shopping malls, Facebook accounts, and Twitter! And, arguably, many males have contributed to this quality of life. Yes, they get credit for that. Well, remember, perception is not necessarily reality.

POP QUIZ

Don't worry it is true/false and self-grading. The quiz is:

<u>ARE THINGS REALLY OKAY, TODAY?</u>

The latest 2016 report by UNICEF showed that 200 million women worldwide have undergone female genital mutilation and the practice is growing. T/F

The Equal Rights Amendment was never ratified into law due in part to actions by a conservative Republican activist from Illinois, Phyllis Schlafly, who threatened EPA would lead to terrible social changes like women in the military and same sex bathrooms.   T/F

Mary Harris Jones (aka Mother Jones), in 1902 was called the most dangerous woman in America because she successfully organized mine workers and their families against mine owners, fighting for safer working conditions, better pay and the introduction of employee benefits. She also fought to implement child labor laws. T/F

The Republican Party, starting with President Ronald Regan through to President Donald Trump, has been systematically destroying labor unions and associated bargaining powers for their workers. T/F

The following companies use child labor: **Nestle', H&M (clothing), Philip Morris, Walmart, Victoria's Secret, The GAP, Apple, Disney, Forever 21, and Hershey.** T/F

More people (**27 million**) live under slavery that any other time in human history. T/F

Human trafficking is the third largest international crime industry (behind illegal drugs and arms trafficking). An estimated 600,000 to 800,000 children, women and men are sold across international borders every year for forced labor or commercial sex. It reportedly generates a **$32 billion yearly profit with $15.5 billion of this profit made in industrialized countries**. T/F

There is an Equal Pay Act of 1963, in the U.S. which prohibits employers from wage discrimination, based on gender, for equal work on jobs requiring equal skill, effort, and responsibility, and performed under similar working conditions. T/F

There still exists an estimated 6% wage gap in the U.S. and a 37% to 50% wage gap worldwide in women's wages as compared to men's. T/F

Approximately 60% of U.S. children living in mother-only families are impoverished, compared with only 11% of two-parent families. T/F

Female infanticide has been practiced since ancient times and is still practiced today, especially in countries where females are considered of low status. T/F

The United Nations has declared that India is the deadliest country for female children, and in 2012 females aged between 1 and 5 years old were 75% more likely to die as opposed to boys. T/F

There were **11 school shootings** in the U.S. in the first **23 days of 2018.** The school shooters were all males. T/F

You're more likely to be shot to death in the United States than you are to die in a car accident in Canada. T/F

There are more than 80,000 chemicals produced and used in the United States. The EPA has been able to require testing on just 200 chemicals, **and only five chemicals have been regulated.** T/F

In a 2005 study, **287 chemicals** and other toxins were found **in the blood of newborn babies**. One pesticide that turned up most was a by-product of DDT (a pesticide banned in 1972). T/F

A Taliban gunman attempted to murder a young Pakistani woman, Malala Yousafzai, because she was an advocate for **women's education and human rights.** She was shot and gravely wounded but survived. Her advocacy has grown into an international movement. T/F

In 2013, the U.S. Supreme Court ruled that naturally occurring genes **could not be patented,** but it allows **edited** or **artificially created DNA** to be patented by the company doing so. T/F

ALL THE STATEMENTS ABOVE ARE TRUE.

If this is truly a "man's world", as the saying goes, then I think we should sue for damages.

19.   THE TRAVAILS OF TIME TRAVEL

Biology is the root difference between female and male brain development. To understand this, we must search far back into our ancestry. We are directly linked to our biological mechanisms for survival. So, this would be a good point to go time-travelling to our ancient ancestral past.

Now before we do, keep in mind that paleoanthropology and archeology are relatively young disciplines and were only established as sciences in the twentieth century. Before that collecting artifacts was a rich man's hobby. We had less than 100 years to establish the rules of study, uncover artifacts and develop methods to analyze the unburied pieces of our past. This is not a very long time and we only know what we *think* we know.

This is different than the physical sciences, like chemistry, where theory had centuries to develop and outcomes are supported by data and verified through testing. The story of the origins of our species tend to change and evolve based on what we last uncovered, and we uncover new stuff all the time.

Currently, scientists recognize that about fifteen to twenty different species of humans once lived on the planet. However, the human species has faced extinction several times resulting in most of these species dying out. The planet has experienced five major extinctions that wiped out an estimated 95%-99% of all life. The last one ended the Cretaceous period, about sixty-six million years ago. That extinction took out the dinosaurs, which was lucky for us. Oh, and yes, scientist believe there is going to be a sixth extinction, but not too soon (we hope).

That said, we categorize ourselves as humanoids because we are bipedal (walk upright on two feet), have complex brains, use language, make and use tools. Now, technically, other species do some of this stuff, too. Apes and even crows use sticks to dig out bugs for eating. Animals have societal structures and communication methods with sounds and body language. Tool-making is what seems to define us the most. The discovery of hand-made tools dates back as far a 3 million years ago. Who these humanoids were, isn't known. Archeologists refer to us as Homo Sapiens. Who we originated from still hasn't been discovered. One group of hominoids considered more primitive and incompatible to Homo Sapiens were the Neanderthals. Only recently, Neanderthal genes have been identified and found to be in our genetic makeup. Who knows who else is swimming in our gene pool?

For our first trip, let's take our time machine back about 75,000 years ago. This is right after our ancestors experienced an extinction threatening event, the super eruption of a volcano in Sumatra. The hole it created is known today as Lake Toba.

Why here? Well, this super eruption would have influenced our behavior as a species. The volcano would have been as damaging as a series of atomic bombs for the region and surrounding areas. It annihilated all life at the site. At the furthest regions from the eruption, the air would have become toxic. Particulates of ash and glasslike shards would be carried in the air across thousands of miles. Breathing these into the lungs would result in painful drawn out deaths for any remaining humans or animals. In the outer regions, ash would cover the land masses, plant life and bodies of water. This would suffocate the plants. Ash landing in water would make it acidic and undrinkable. It would kill marine and aquatic life.

Only the furthest areas from the volcano would be tolerable for life. But the vast amount of air pollutants would impact the atmosphere. Sunlight would be blocked from the planet's surface causing a prolonged mini-ice age. Plants can't grow, animals starve, and many species die off. The humanoids who depended on the plants and animals to live, would suffer, too.

It isn't known how many humans died, but the times would favor those with aggressive and even violent behavior. Those who could fight and claim a territory favorable to survival could survive. Aggressive control of food and water sources may increase the chance of living. There is evidence of cannibalism from markings on bones from ancient times. This indicates how desperate conditions were for the surviving humans. Being brutal in this harsh and primitive setting could increase species survival. Unfortunately, the survival of the most aggressive also means those genes were carried into future generations.

Now, let's move our time machine to around ten thousand years ago. We refer to these humans as our hunter-gatherer ancestors. They are still living in a physically harsh world, but some conditions have improved since the super eruption.

The worldwide human population at this time is estimated to be around ten thousand humans. This low population suggests times are still very tough. Humans would be suffering from food shortages and facing periods of starvation. Groups that encounter each other may find themselves in competition for resources. Despite their small numbers, harsh conditions may have caused our ancient ancestors to create and engaged in the action we know as 'war'.

20.   THE NATARUK MASSACRE

Yup, war was invented as far back as 10,000 years ago. We tend to view our ancestors from a modern, somewhat sanitized perspective. Hunter-gatherers were originally thought of as shy and gentle folk, like Hobbits of the Shire. Not so, they had learned to survive through aggressive measures and were just as violent as chimpanzees. Evidence of this behavior comes from a discovery described as a 10,000-year-old "massacre" of hunter-gatherers, uncovered in 2012 at Nataruk, near Lake Turkana in Kenya.

The remains of at least twenty-seven people, unburied and exposed to the elements were uncovered. It was assumed that one group of hunter-gatherers had attacked and slaughtered another. The dead had crushed skulls, and were embedded with arrow or spear points, along with other devastating wounds. There was no attempt at burial, they were just left as they lay. Twelve of the skeletons were relatively complete and ten skeletons showed unmistakable signs of violent death. Partial remains of at least fifteen other people were found at the site. They were all thought to have died in the same attack.

Forensic study of the bones showed that one man had head injuries from arrows or small spears and was clubbed in the knee. A woman, pregnant with a six- to nine-month-old fetus, was killed by a blow to the head. The fetal skeleton was still in her abdominal region. Furthermore, the position of her hands and feet suggested that she may have been tied up before she was killed. Given that only the most aggressive and violent males (and females) survived in the harsh world of the hunter-gatherer, these findings should have been no surprise. But we don't like to think of our ancestors, whose genes we carry, behaving this way.

Violence has always been part of human behavior. But, for some reason, the origins of war are hotly debated. Some experts try to explain it as deeply rooted in evolution, pointing to violent interactions among groups of chimpanzees as clues to an ancestral predilection. Others emphasize the influence of complex and hierarchical human societies that practice rape and pillage for wealth and food as the excuse. These are the effects, but the cause is much simpler. Fear.

Violence is a direct result of a core emotion that is in all species. Fear. It is fear of death and the drive to survive. The actions of "fight or flight" are hot-wired in the brains of all living things. If you are alive today, thank your ancestor's amygdala. They are two almond-shaped sections of nervous tissue located in each side of the brain around the area of your ears. These are responsible for emotions, survival instincts, and memory. Think of these as part of your lizard brain. It operates on emotion, no rational thought or filters, is only interested in basic survival and remembers with positive/negative reinforcement. Kind of like how lizards operate.

So, if you are a starving hunter-gatherer and you run across someone who has food, what are your options? Flight gets you nothing, but fighting might get you fed. You don't consider the other person except as an obstacle to getting food. This inherited aggressiveness is alive and well today. Luckily, it isn't the only gene pool we swim in for our behavior.

When circumstances are extreme and threatening, two mutant male characteristics seem to emerge. One group are males who provide help, try to secure the safety of others and provide aid to those in need. The other group of mutant males is made up of those who ignore the crisis or take advantage of the chaos to get what they want and even threaten or take advantage of the vulnerable.

21.　　　A HUNTER GATHERING, WE GO

It is important to remember that these humans may have resembled us, but they were still in the early stages of self-awareness. Identity was just developing in concept for individuals and groups. Emotional behavior in relation to rational thought, was still being worked out. Neither emotions or thinking were fully defined or understood. Everything was learned through trial and error. Relationships were basic. Pairings were with those who were convenient or similar. Social skills were rudimentary if they existed. The notion of good or bad may have just started to evolve. Morality, ethics, and standards were fairly non-existent. These were not stupid people, rather they might be viewed by us as mildly autistic in behavior.

For our hunter-gatherer ancestors, aggressive tendencies were more than likely normal behavior which helped keep the male and female alive. The female had to share survival characteristics and be aggressive as well. As a pair, they both functioned equally, and their primary focus was survival. As rather vulnerable humans in the harsh natural world, both genders hunted together for food, usually small rodents, and foraged for plants, roots, grasses, berries and fruits.

The hot-wiring in the human brain created the tendency of both genders to be attracted to each other. Long-term pairings may have been supported by the fact that there weren't that many people around. If you found a mate, you might consider yourself lucky. Sticking together assured a better chance for survival. Even today, most people have a fear of being alone. Regardless of pride in your intellect and associated achievements, your human brain and body are still running the show. You are still operating towards these two basic goals: to stay alive and continue the species.

In other words, your biology doesn't care about your ego or how educated, rich or famous you are, your body just wants to eat, drink, sleep, be safe and procreate. Of course, being educated and rich does help you achieve these things more easily. If you could provide your body with these needs by living out of a dumpster, it would be just as happy. I'm only guessing about this. You'd have to ask the 100 million homeless if that is true or not.

22.   HOORAY FOR THE GOOD MOMMY AND DADDY GENES

For all practical purposes, the birth of a baby, in the world of the hunter-gatherer was a life-threatening burden to the female and a danger to the pair's survival. A baby is noisy and smelly. With birth, there is blood. These things attract predators. So, good 'daddy' genes helped the family, thus species, to survive. That is, the male didn't just think, 'forget this', and walk away. He stayed, kept guard and maybe helped.

Also, the baby does not contribute to finding food. Instead, it requires constant feeding and attention. The baby drains the female of her nutrients, daily, by feeding off her. If their surroundings have ample food sources, this isn't too much of a problem. But, ample food also attracts animals or other humans to the location; and predators are attracted to smelly, noisy babies.

Based on their need to survive, once the female expelled the noisy, smelly baby from her body, the pair should just abandon it. As a side note, try to imagine the female's emotional and physical state after enduring pregnancy, and experiencing the trauma of giving birth? Once a female experiences this, she'd remember everything about it and, she might do anything to avoid the experience again. To offset this the female brain tends to 'forget' childbirth trauma. Biology also takes over and controls the female regarding the infant. Her brain is hot-wired to be attracted to the noise an infant makes, to be empathetic to the baby, to want to nurture it and keep it.

This isn't what the male feels, however. The survival of the infant isn't his priority. He might prefer to leave it behind because of his survival instinct. The male practice of infant abandonment has been demonstrated throughout history. Even today, males will abandon their female partners and their children if their basic survival feels threatened. And just like in primitive times, this risks the children's success for survival. (Remember the one in five children living in poverty, today.) This is where the strength of the pair's bond is tested and determines the outcome of the situation. Think about it, if babies were routinely abandoned, well, that's the end of the gene pool. Most of us would not exist today.

Ironically, the stronger the pair bond, the greater the likelihood that the male's genes continue into future generations. An interesting dilemma for the male; learn to bond and be protective, but also aggressively seek survival options and be violent when needed.

Now, don't think the female behaved perfectly, either. Females would have abandoned or killed their off-spring in survival situations, perhaps, prompted by the male. Sort of like, "Saber toothed tiger attack! Drop everything (including baby) and run for your life!" Babies didn't have much value. Remember Sparta with its "toss a baby off a cliff" practice. Many ancient cultures, like the Romans, would leave their unwanted infants, mostly girls, exposed to die. Many ancient cultures even used babies and children for religious ceremonial sacrifice. Why? They were expendable in patriarchal cultures. Even today, children are sold into slavery.

Males are not the life-givers, they do not experience pregnancy nor are their brains wired for nurturing. Nurturing is the strongest and most successful female trait. Humans that protected their off-spring increased the chances of their gene pool being carried forward. So, good mommy and daddy genes usually got carried forward.

Biology imposes a great burden on the female, but also gives the female brain extra abilities to deal with this burden. How so? Back to our primitive mother. By now, there may be two off-spring, because the male has good daddy genes and the bond is strong and working. The male brain is developing traits of linear focus, such as find food, find water, find safe shelter, etc. The male brain is getting good at accomplishing these singular tasks.

But the female brain is developing differently. It must be different to nurture and support the off-spring. With two off-spring, the female mind learns complex, multi-leveled thought processes. It develops ways to see inter-connected relationships, create communication skills and accomplish multiple tasks within a short timeframe.

For example, mommy hunter-gatherer (HG) must carry the newest baby, keep track of the toddler and her mate. Toddler HG roams around, explores and looks for food. Mommy HG creates a vocal way to communicate with the active toddler. It becomes more complex than needed with her mate. Toddler HG is curious and sticks things in her/his mouth, wanders away, falls, cries, and is generally chaos on two little feet. Mommy HG can't chase after her/him with the baby in her arms. That's exhausting. Take care of a toddler for a day and see if you do not go home tired.

Mommy HG creates a variety of sounds that have a range of information. These basic communications would be something like: "Yes, eat the bug," or "No, spit that out". "Come here", "Quiet!", "Danger", "Stand still." or "Run." There would be comforting or soothing sounds, too. Some ancient female began a vocabulary of sounds to tell her toddler about food and how to keep safe. She also had to remember what she said to be consistent. These sounds would be passed on to the future generations through her off-springs. Language!

Generally, Mommy HG must be on constant alert, monitoring conditions around her, watching for toddler, for predators and other dangers, scanning the ground for food, nursing and monitoring the baby and trying to keep the kids quiet. In addition, she must keep her mate in sight and watch his body language for signs of danger. Add to this, her developing a memory that identifies which plants were edible, and other critical survival information. Well, you get the idea. Multi-tasking. The female brain had to become more complex than the male's due to the demands of creating, nurturing and supporting off-spring while trying to keep herself safe and alive.

As mentioned, the female was just as capable as the male until she got pregnant and had to support her off-spring. This biological "burden", handicapped the female physically because as pregnancy progressed it weakened the female. This biological burden would have slowly formed a social and cultural perception towards the female in the male mind. Depending upon the nature of the group dynamic, the attitude would be of either support or prejudice against the female. In other words, "pregnancy weakness" may have become the stigma of "female weakness", imposed on the gender throughout history and resulted in the female's diminished social status.

Even today, care-givers are less socially valued when compared to bread-winners. Because food gathering was of primary importance, this shift in responsibilities allowed the male to gain an upper hand and a favored or elevated position within the early forming social groups. Was, the "Me, Big Hunter" attitude how human male vanity developed, or has it always been part of the male psyche?

23.   YOUR ARE YOUR BIOLOGY, YOU ARE YOUR BRAIN

The biology of each gender created two different brains. The male hunter-gatherer's brain is basically focused on survival. The female's brain is more complicated. She is the creator of the next generation. This is an enormous burden. The brain must oversee her physical changes for pregnancy. It must monitor the stages of pregnancy and release the right biochemicals into her bloodstream in the right amounts and during the exact time needed by the fetus.

It is a myth that humans use only 10% of their brain, they use 100%. The male who came up with that idea failed to realize that nature never wastes space. Giving you a three-pound brain, wrapped in a densely protective skull with an energy consumption equivalent to a 15-watt bulb, comprised of one hundred billion nerve cells and the hardwiring of one thousand times one billion nerve cell connections, wasn't a whim of Mother Nature. The author of the myth may only use 10% of his thinking ability, but your brain uses 100% of its capacity to keep the body alive and well.

Making a baby kicks female brains into overdrive. Baby development and health depends on the health of the mom's brain. That's why many pregnant females go through periods where they have difficulty thinking, are tired, and emotional. It means parts of mom's brain aren't working well and have some damage. The symptoms show that her brain it is trying to compensate by taking blood and energy from the cognitive (thinking) part of the brain and sending them to the "baby making" parts of the brain.

In his book, "We Are Our Brains", Dutch physician and neuroscientist D.F. Swaab, gives a readable summary of his 30 years of brain research which explains how complex this organ really is and its relationship with our health and bodies. For example, there are small areas deep within the female brain dedicated primarily to activities of the uterus and other parts dedicated to embryonic/fetal development. If they are damaged, it won't show up until a pregnancy occurs. And, we all have brain damage, but where and how much can't be known until we need that part of the brain.

Sadly, yes, our brains are damaged. Remember Chapter 11 on environmental toxins? Let's explore that a bit more. Since everyone is carrying a toxic burden in the blood and 20% of your blood is used by the brain, then those toxins are in your brain. I am focusing this chapter on pregnancy, but there is a good probability that toxins are causing many health problems, both mental and physical in our population. Imagine what health and mental conditions those born with toxins already in their blood will have to cope with during their life.

The human brain is so complex it does not fully mature until twenty-five years of age. That is a very long time for a biological organ to develop. During this time the brain is still forming important parts of itself. The toxins it is dealing with easily interfere with healthy development and can damage cells. The brain may end up with scar tissue where it needs healthy tissue. Toxins can even prevent parts of the brain from growing as they should. In the female, if this happens, it is possible that the damaged parts of her brain, such as the sections that monitor the growth of her fetus, won't work as they should. The good news is that the brain is constantly trying to compensate and find alternative ways to fix itself. But if it can't, here are some examples of what could happen.

If mom's brain isn't properly supporting the embryo's development it can cause problems with organ development, especially brain and spine development (first trimester). The spinal canal may fail to close completely around the spinal cord. In the second trimester, a fetal organ may fail to perform properly, due to the failure of mom's brain to provide the right biochemical triggers. This can result in faulty heart, liver or kidney development. The third trimester is where the fetus's brain to body connection occurs. If the fetal brain is receiving the wrong hormonal amounts, it may fail to relate to the gender of its physical body. Too much estrogen during this critical period causes a male to identify as female and the opposite is true. Too much testosterone causes a female brain to identify as male. This is what happens when people have gender dysphoria and say they are "trapped in the wrong body."

Many young females (and males) fail to understand how important their life-long (brain) health is if they plan to have children. There is a tendency for young people to believe they are invincible. They engage in smoking, drinking and the use of drugs thinking there are no consequences. Unfortunately, this behavior damages their brains. Young people are too immature to realize the damage they are doing to their brains and bodies. The damage affects their cognitive ability to rationally consider the costs of their actions on their health. So, they create a cycle of self-destruction by continuing to abuse their bodies. Add the toxic body burden from the environment and it is no wonder that the average Western Intelligence Quotient (IQ) has dropped 14 points over the last century. It is official, we are getting dumber.

24.   TOXIC MUTANT MALE VERSUS MARVELOUS MUTANT MALE

As hunter-gatherer groups formed into tribes, the males experienced new stressors. And as shown by our little Siberian foxes, behavior alters form, which alters behavior. So, did socialized groupings create other genetic differences? Males couldn't be violent and aggressive within their own tribe without causing problems. They had to change to be accepted within the group. This might be when harmonious males or nice guys started to show up. Males who were more balanced and cooperative were a marvel, since they had to evolve within an environment dominated by their toxic compatriots. Remember our culture has a "nice guys finish last" theory. Well, somehow, the nice guys managed to integrate both their male and female traits in their behavior within the group and survive. They were marvels!

A supportive social setting eases the stress of daily survival. Males can relax a bit and get in touch with their other (female) traits, such as empathy, creativity and communication. Remember males are originally female which means they carry these characteristics as part of their genetic makeup.

Of course, if the social environment is harsh, the aggressor traits or tendencies stay as a part of the male personae. There may be group social pressure for the male to be a "man". Man would be defined by whatever standards the most aggressive male(s) exhibits and promotes. Think of the Vikings or the Huns as examples. The gene pool will continue with aggression as a strong characteristic, but within the tribe, males learn to get along with each other. Behavior will slowly alter aggressive characteristics into those of cooperation and collaboration (female traits). Cultural attitudes towards the female would either continue with (good daddy) protector traits or devolve into domination and control of the female. Curiously, the fewer number of valued females available for mating, the more domination and control impulses emerge as male traits.

Stress to provide for the family within a hierarchical group may cause problems too. If a male is low in status within a group, it stresses his vanity. Violence may grow within a domestic pairing because it is convenient to take one's frustrations out on a dependent, vulnerable partner. If the male isn't a particularly talented hunter, the burden of finding food and the social implications of failure could cause resentment. To compensate for injured male vanity, he might shove his female's status further down the social ladder with the justification that she doesn't hunt.

Any combination of factors, may have laid the groundwork for patriarchal social structures of developing civilizations. This is just theory. But, the prevalence of gender bigotry is not and unfortunately, in the twenty-first century, males continue the practice of domestic violence as if it were the year 800 B.C. In many countries violence against the female isn't even recognized as a crime. A United Nations report estimates that six hundred million women experience domestic violence, worldwide. If this is not mutant behavior, what is?

25.   TESTOSTERONE TOXICITY

I would like to introduce the idea of "testosterone toxicity". This male hormone, testosterone, promotes the emotional and physical male characteristics such as strength, independence, competition, and aggression, among others. These can be seen both positively or negatively depending upon circumstances. When in excess testosterone can trigger aggressive and abusive behavior. That is why male animals are often neutered, it makes them nicer to deal with and safer to be around. No, I am not advocating neutering human males.....okay, not yet. Joke!

Mutant males can be toxic in ways other than just physical brutality. Toxic mutants can display selfishness, deception, greed, arrogance, lack of empathy, lack of accountability, lack of morality, narcissism, laziness and treachery. The problem is that many of these behaviors are tolerated in the mutant male of today. Some toxic traits have even become celebrated. They represent standards of expected behavior within certain organizations, like corporations, the military, professional sports and governments. These are the "boys" clubs of society.

Tolerating and accepting destructive mutant male behavior as a standard undermines the progress we are working towards in civilizing ourselves. There is a saying, "Among cannibals, cannibalism is considered normal." The subtle meaning of this statement is that tolerating toxic behavior normalizes it and makes it acceptable.

26. SAVE US ALL FROM MALE VANITY

The most damaging and damning result of this hormone is male vanity. It is the cause of all the world's woes. Any action is permissible that supports the male's conceit about deserving it all. Kings, emperors and dictators have killed hundreds of thousands because they wanted more land, titles or wealth. The male's arrogant claim of righteousness in religious authorities has supported torture and genocide. The male belief in his superiority encouraged imperialism and condoned slavery. All behavior is acceptable, as long as it satisfies the mutant male's vanity.

Another example of the dangers of male vanity is, that if a male feels alienated from society, he blames society and acts out against it. He rationalizes that all his problems are 'their' fault. Basically, his ego does not allow for self-assessment. He may not consider that he is part of the problem.

This is one of the ways terrorists are recruited. The recruiters manipulate the male's wounded ego. They puff up his pride. Using terms like hero, martyr, righteous defender, etc., they inflate his self-image. Manipulating the vanity of these males is so effective that young men are willing to strap explosives on themselves to kill innocent people. How mutant is the thinking of these males to believe that this destructive action will gain them prestige and a booty call (seventy-two virgins, seriously?). What they actually gain is a doggy-bag filled with whatever is left of their remains after they are scrapped up off the sidewalk.

Also, consider how toxic the mutant male(s) is who callously manipulates a susceptible young person into carrying out this violent self-destructive act. That the basic human instinct for survival is overridden by male vanity demonstrates the power of this conceit. Toxicity breeds toxicity.

In contrast, most females who feel alienated tend to blame themselves and may even do self-harm. This is in part due to the brainwashing of a male dominated society that imposes fault on the female for just about everything.

As an example, rape victims, historically and even now, are blamed for provoking rape behavior in males because of their dress, behavior or attractiveness. This punitive attitude is alive and well even in the twenty-first century. Unbelievably, in some countries, the women who are raped are not only punished for inciting the rape, but also punished for being raped because they are no longer considered "pure" after being violated. This is mutant male thinking at its most vile.

27. THE GENDER POLITICS OF RELIGION

Recognizing that the male is a mutation raises questions about the origins of religious dogma. For example, the story of Adam and Eve. It is biologically wrong. Quite frankly, the man/men who wrote the stories, which were based on ancient mythologies, knew nothing about biology, DNA or how babies were made. And, since they were mutant males with their associated gender bias and immense (mutant) male egos, they wrote a version of themselves as the omnipresent or divine power model. In other words, as has always been suspected, man created god in his own image.

One mutant male teacher who was well balanced in thought and action was Joshua bin Joseph. He is mistakenly referred to as "Jesus Christ" which is a Greek title meaning "anointed messiah". This evolved male and all round nice guy, was a marvel because he taught tolerance, forgiveness, sharing and respect for life. Joshua was a socialist who disdained wealth, privilege and viewed both men and women as equals. To the Hebrews and Romans of his time, with their patriarchal values of wealth, dominance and power, this was total sacrilege. No wonder they crucified him. By the way, can you imagine what they would have done to a female if she had tried to teach the same values? After his death, his very simple lessons were distorted into a thick tome of rigid dogma.

Today, patriarchal religions all seem to plagiarize his words, distorting them into mutant male propaganda. Tolerance is replaced with bigotry and prejudice. "Keeping up with the Jones", has replaced "love they neighbor. Anyone who is different is not welcome, they are suspect, even dangerous. Spirituality isn't between you and your divinity, instead, it belongs to an authoritarian (generally male) go-between who has a privileged Twitter account with the divine. Equality means belonging to a select group, class and gender. And, the new manna from heaven is wealth and the acquisition of things, lots of things.

Curiously, one primary corruption of Joshua's teachings was the belief that if you are rich, it is because God loves you. If you are poor, it is because he doesn't. He never taught that idea, in fact, he taught that the opposite was true. Pursuit of wealth and the acquisition of stuff represents a failure of spiritual development. He taught that physical acquisitions are a transitory illusion.

But, by the sixteen-century, the Puritans had embraced the wealth dogma with gusto, editing their preaching to fit their (greedy) needs. They transplanted this new religion in the, so called, new world with great success. Even today, many modern Evangelical ministers preach this idea with great monetary benefit to themselves. It infects the Wall Street stock exchange, corporations and government who all revel in the belief that "greed is good". Again, this is not what Joshua bin Joseph taught. He was a man that distained privilege, prestige, wealth and power. People who claim they follow his teachings forget the very substance of his teachings. Remember all the healings he gave? He was the first person to give free healthcare. He would probably be arrested today for practicing medicine without a license.

The biological fact is that the female is the life giver. The male was mutated for the biological purpose of diversity but does not produce and support new life. Males can't nurse, remember their non-functioning nipples. So, going back to the idea of a divine male life-giver is in total contradiction to biological reality and to nature. Just because mutant males of ancient times insisted on marketing their prejudicial viewpoints as facts, doesn't change this reality. Those misogynistic old men, knowing nothing of biology, wove a fictional tale describing life and its origin with the specific purpose of supporting their male elitism. If you are wondering what religion I am referring to, well, just take your pick, because they are all guilty of prejudice and gender bigotry.

Religion is not spirituality. Religion emerged as a needed control over disruptive human behaviors. You know, the ones mutant males exhibit. Yet, because religions are the domain of mutant males, they all exhibit mutant male tendencies such as the persecution and killing of more people than can be known. Religious dogma has justified torture and killing as methods for cleansing society of nonbelievers. Is it really that hard to have a simple philosophy that respects life, in all its forms? The truly great spiritual teachers promoted this simple idea. Anything beyond this is propaganda serving a secular agenda with the aim of making some smooth talkers (both male and female) very rich.

Overall, divinity as described by mutant males, has resembled and favored the male. But, by doing so, it cemented future social foundations with gender bias against the female. This prejudice has seeped into every aspect of thought, attitude and behavior towards females. It laid the groundwork for centuries of repression and is fostering a dangerous and even deadly prejudice towards females even today. Modern studies in human genetics exposes this fiction. But can mutant male vanity accept the facts? Also, given the current state of self-awareness of the human species, it is obvious that whatever created this universe is far beyond our abilities to comprehend. Remember, we just lost 14 points in our collective IQ's.

28. THE INMATES ARE RUNNING THE ASYLUM

The fact that males are genetic mutants should raise many questions. For example, we should question the whole array of mutant male values, standards and judgements (which have directed and controlled social development). These should be carefully examined, especially now in the twenty-first century.

Popular media reflects cultural norms. In most movies males are still represented as aggressive and violent, even if they are the "heroes". The media message is that, to be male, one must show superiority with brutality, aggression and killing. Many of today's popular video games are about war, violence and murder, with very detailed graphics including blood splatter and mutilation.

Currently, so called "leaders" worldwide engage in typical male "pissing" contests. Their use of threats and actual military force, punitive sanctions and invasion is the mutant males' way of showing dominance. Again, it is all about male vanity. It is all about forcing one's will upon another. The "Biggus Dickus" syndrome. Even in international negotiations, competitive tactics emerge in their verbal exchanges. These divisive attitudes are so deeply engrained in the male psyche, it is almost impossible to imagine their discussions without these negative influences. This shows that there are no true leaders in this world. Because real leaders of true greatness realize that competition destroys communication. And, without communication, there can be no negotiation and no cooperation.

The pretenses toxic mutant males use to support their need for control are patriotism, religion, racial superiority, resource control, social advantage and economic security. Toxic mutant male perceptions are all designed to justify aggression or violence. This viewpoint promotes actions of threat, assault, destruction and death. They are good at marketing the concept to others that the lives of hundreds of thousands of human beings and the suffering of many more is worth the loss provided it satiates the needs of toxic mutant male vanity. Remember Adolf Hitler, Joseph Stalin, and Harry Truman?

Life is inconsequential to the toxic mutant male, unless it is his own. Consequences of violence and brutality are immaterial. The destruction of cities, social orders and human lives is justified, as long as it is the "others" that suffer and the toxic mutant male gets what he wants. This is the predominate worldwide attitude existing today promoted by the mutant males. It helps support this ongoing sociopathy. To paraphrase the words of the song, "The Universal Soldier", written by the singer, Donovan, "(the mutant male) knows he shouldn't kill, but, he knows he always will." War is not the way to end war.

Should this seem a wee bit harsh, here is a brief summary of the consequences of toxic mutant male actions. The following is a snapshot of worldwide current conflicts and their estimated death tolls.

War in Afghanistan
149,000 deaths.

War in Iraq
4,424 total deaths

Desert Storm

100,000 Iraqi deaths and 383 American deaths

War in North-West Pakistan, estimated
173,000 deaths

Somali Civil War,
500,000 deaths

Liberian Civil War
250,000 deaths

American-led Intervention in Iraq
500,000 deaths (2003-2013)

Syria
481,612 deaths

Mexican Drug War
106,000 deaths

In fact, for the past three thousand, four hundred years of humans' existence, it is estimated that peace was experienced for only a total of two hundred and sixty-eight years or just 8% of recorded history. An estimated one hundred and eight million people were killed in wars in the twentieth century alone. The total number of people killed in wars for all human history is estimated to be from one hundred, fifty million to one billion. In fact, in the twenty-first century, out of the 195 countries of the world, only 11 countries are free from conflict. Perhaps, this is the toxic mutant male's idea for population control? Wouldn't Planned Parenthood be a better option?"

Now consider this, every single death represents a sacrifice by a woman. A woman went through pregnancy, delivery and nurturing of her baby. She committed her time, made both physical and emotional investments and, in many cases, forfeited her economic status to support her child. There is no value for her sacrifice. The only value recognized is the income gained by the instigators of each conflict. War is profitable. There are over one hundred military contractors selling the U.S. government arms and military services costing the people four hundred, ten billion dollars. Their interests are the primary reason the U.S. is invested in military spending.

Whether the death tolls represent soldiers or civilians, adults or children, the loss means nothing to these mutant males or their government lackies. You may argue these deaths are also losses for the fathers. But, the mutant male mindset cushions his loss by creating medals and ceremonies to "honor" the dead. This is mutant male brainwashing. Medals and empty platitudes are not the equivalent of a human life.

Toxic mutant male attitudes only reward male aspects, traits, characteristics and behaviors. Ambition, competition, aggression, strength, wealth and control is the ultimate achievement. That is why the toxic mutant male has no respect for life. This isn't just a lack of respect for human life. It is a lack of respect for all life and a disregard of the very biosphere that supports all life on (Mother) earth.

The earth's biosphere is composed of the living organisms on the planet, plants, animals, bacteria, fungi and even single-celled organisms. All these species are interconnected and have established symbiotic relationships. Trees produce oxygen and clean the air, plants feed animals, bees pollinate plants, birds keep insect populations in check and spread seeds, predatory animals keep herbivores in check and so on. All life follows a cycle of life, death, decay, resulting in rejuvenation and new life. These cycles maintain the biosphere. There is no symbiosis in the actions of the mutant male. The majority of activities the mutant male engages in is for male vanity, profit or control.

Too harsh again? Look how cities have been created and what environments they support. Do they help renew the biosphere or do they create garbage and pollution? What about the way natural resources are extracted to support these cities with their energy needs. Oil drilling, fracking and petroleum production are destructive to the biosphere and environment. There is no symbiotic relationship between male-made cities and the biosphere. As far as humans are concerned, it is all 'take' and no give.

Do you remember about the toxins in your blood and body? It is from the processing methods used to make all the products marketed to you for profit as "must-haves" and "needs". What about the destruction of thousands of acres of tropical rain forests and old growth forests to grow palm oil, soy beans, beef cattle or rubber trees. These forests are the ecosystems that help create oxygen and clean the air. You know, the stuff you breathe. The destruction of these ecosystems is motivated by greed for wealth. But the wealth is for the few at the expense of everyone. None of these actions provides a relationship that helps the renewal of the biosphere. They just provide multiple deposits to the bank accounts of corporate toxic mutant males. Destruction of the biosphere is the destruction of the support system of life on this planet.

29.   MUTANT MALES ON MARS

In typical mutant male fashion, the solution for all the destruction they have created is to run away from the problem. Let's all move to Mars. Well, although the movies have made it look fairly easy, remember, you were created on this planet, not on Mars.

Earth is far superior to Mars. First, Earth is alive. Mars is dead. Earth has an active energy core, Mars does not. Earth has a biosphere that supports live that has taken trillions of years to develop. Mars does not. Even if it were possible to get the needed technology, energy sources, and materials transferred to Mars, it will take a very long time before anything resembling terraforming could take place, if that was even possible.

Earth is surrounded with a thin protective blanket of gases called the atmosphere. This complex atmosphere is made up of 78% nitrogen, 21% oxygen, 0.9% argon, and 0.03% carbon dioxide with very small percentages of other elements and water vapor. Earth has an ozone layer. It protects life from the sun's harmful rays. It also acts as a buffer for space debris. Meteors entering this layer generally burn up, which protects the earth's surface. Both the ozone and atmospheric layers help modify extreme temperature changes. Humans seem determined to destroy the earth's protective layers through atmospheric pollution. The atmosphere of Mars is about 100 times thinner than Earth's and it is 95% carbon dioxide. Go ahead, take a deep breathe.

The Earth's mantle is made up of rock containing silicon, iron, magnesium, aluminum, oxygen and other minerals. A thin layer of complex, organic matter and living organisms make up what we call soil which covers the mantle, supporting plant and animal life. The dust that covers the surface of Mars is fine talcum-like powder. Beneath this layer of dust, the Martian crust consists mostly of volcanic basalt rock. The dirt of Mars also holds nutrients such as sodium, potassium, chloride and magnesium. But, don't get too excited about this, chemicals do not soil make.

Soil is the result of a slow but constant cyclic interaction of organic materials, air, water and living organisms. Matt Damon's poop potatoes, as seen in the movie, "The Martian" are not very plausible. Besides, Matt would have suffered from malnutrition on a diet of poop potatoes within a few months of living on Mars.

Earth also has something Mars does not, the Van Allen radiation belts. This is a zone of energetically charged particles, most of which originate from solar wind, from the sun. This wind of radiation particles is captured by and held around the planet by Earth's magnetic field. The two main belts extend from an altitude of about 500 to 58,000 kilometers above the planet's surface

Mars has no inner dynamo to create a major global magnetic field. The Martian magnetosphere is less extensive than Earth's. This means Mars has a very poor magnetosphere or shield to prevent solar wind charged particles from reaching the planet's surface. Life on Mars would be constantly exposed to high radiation levels and severe atmosphere changes.

Lastly, toxic mutant males will take with them the same destructive traits, no matter where they go. The fault is not with Earth, the fault and failure are that of the testosterone toxic mutant male.

Ready to move to Mars?

30. SO WHY DOES ALL THIS MATTER?

Why does this matter? Does life matter? The toxic mutant males are behaving as if they still live in the primitive conditions of our hunter-gatherer ancestors. They threaten life on this planet. They still want to club each other over the head, hoard all the food (and wealth) for themselves, and act without accountability for their actions. But, now, their actions have negative global consequences, many of which are non-reversible in their destructive nature.

Today, nuclear weapons have replaced clubs and spears. Worldwide wealth is controlled by 1% of the world's population, meanwhile roughly 12% of the world's population starve and go without basic needs. Decimation of air, water and soil, our biosphere, is a routine practice of corporate cultures in the name of profits.

Furthermore, mutant males manipulate laws and glory in the corruption of governments to satiate their male vanities. Mutant male brainwashing influences social attitudes through the media and marketing. It would take another book to list all the negative effects of testosterone toxic mutant males.

In the nineteenth-century industrialists (or robber barons) such as, J.P. Morgan, Andrew Carnegie, Andrew W. Mellon, and John D. Rockefeller used unscrupulous methods to get rich, much like corporations do today. These "captains of industry" exploited natural resources, corrupted legislators, and worked their employees up to sixteen hours a day and six days a week. Industries employed children as young as four years old to work twelve- to fourteen-hour days, in dangerous conditions. There were no benefits, sick leave, holiday pay, workplace safety, coverage for injuries or death on the job.

Women, such as Mary Harris Jones (Mother Jones), fought against these industrialists to create fair labor laws to protect the worker and establish child labor laws. These women were able to change the working conditions and gain rights for the working class, despite having no voting rights or legal status themselves under nineteenth century laws and government.

Don't you think it is time to correct the current accumulation of insults and injuries that still exist, not just against half the population of humanity, but for the whole human race and the planet on which we live. Isn't it time to hold toxic mutant males accountable for their actions? Isn't it time to take control of the asylum out of the hands of the inmates?

On January 21, 2017, a worldwide event took place called, The Women's March. It started simply by Teresa Shook of Hawaii creating a Facebook event to invite friends to march on Washington. This became a worldwide movement to advocate legislation and policies regarding human rights and other issues, including women's rights, immigration reform, and support of healthcare. Similar Facebook pages created by Evie Harmon, Fontaine Pearson, Bob Bland (a New York fashion designer), Breanne Butler, and others quickly led to thousands of women signing up to march. Harmon, Pearson, and Butler united their efforts by consolidating their pages, beginning the official Women's March on Washington. Women of differing races and backgrounds were included with the help of Vanessa Wruble, co-founder, and co-president of OkayAfrica. Tamika D. Mallory, Carmen Perez and Linda Sarsour served as National Co-Chairs alongside Bland. Janaye Ingram, a former Miss New Jersey, served as Head of Logistics and filmmaker, Paola Mendoza served as Artistic Director and a National Organizer.

The momentum, scope and diversity of this movement shows what females, who care, can do. It was just as dynamic as the actions of Mother Jones. The nature of the female is about supporting and promoting the importance of life. Their march was not just about female issues, it was about the condition of human beings worldwide. Thousands raised their voice in unison. This cooperative communication declared for everyone who was oppressed, disenfranchised, forgotten, and vulnerable. It was a call for change, and continued action must follow.

As females and males realize how their influence can affect change, they may be motivated to continue promoting actions that stop and even reverse the damage done by a multitude of wrongs created by toxic mutant males. Not just females, but everyone who respects life, must do what they can to help heal ourselves and our world. Hopefully, before it is too late. *Because time is short and the water's rising.*

31. YOU ARE EITHER A PART OF THE SOLUTION OR A PART OF THE PROBLEM!

Yes, there are many real good, marvelous (still mutant) males in the world. I will even list a few who should be male role models:

- Mahatma Gandhi,
- The Dali Lama
- Joshua bin Joseph
- Martin Luther King, Jr.,
- Nelson Mandela,
- John Walsh,
- Oskar Schindler,
- Per Anger,
- Norman Borlaug,
- Johns Hopkins
- Sir Nicholas Winton (Wertheim)
- Dr. Thomas Anthony Dooley III

- Paul Newman.

Feel free to "Google" their names for more information on why they are "marvelous" mutant males.

Here are a few female role models:

- Mother Teresa,
- Mary Harris Jones,
- Harriet Tubman,
- Charlotte E. Ray,
- Maya Angelou,
- Oprah Winfrey,
- Malala Yousafzai,
- Octavia E. Butler,
- Shirley Chisholm,
- Jane Addams,
- Dorothea Dix,
- Lucretia Mott,
- Josephine Butler.
- Noella Coursaris Musunka,
- Carolyn Rafaelian,
- Leila Janah,
- Hypatia of Alexandria,
- Margaret Cavendish,
- Marie Paulze Lavoisie,
- Sophie Germain,
- Margaret Sanger, and
- Anne Conway, to name a few.

Consider this, females are fifty percent of the population. This means that over the millennia of human development half the human species has been denied opportunities that may have contributed towards the improvement of the human condition. Yet, the females above, despite this oppression, made substantial social changes that contributed to improved conditions for many human lives.

Female attitudes have been omitted or ignored in the formation of cities, governments, religions, social structures, writing and even art. If the female were allowed equal participation in matters, if her thinking and viewpoint were respected, if her voice was heard, would the world, still be (as said by the young child, earlier) a "messed up place"? Or, would female contributions have made a substantial impact towards creating a better, safer world? Instead of *his*tory or *her*story, the human species could be telling "ourstory".

32.   THE TESTOSTERONE TOXIC MUTANT MALE IS EVERYWHERE!

I want to provide some short lists of those who should be noted for their mutant male toxicity: I am sure I am missing many, many males from this list, so, feel free to make your own lists.

Those responsible for the pending decline and fall of the United States of America:

Republican Party members: specifically,

- Mitch McConnell,
- Paul Ryan,
- Jess Sessions and, of course,
- President Donald Trump.

- Special shout out to all those in the U.S. congress who refused to pass much needed laws on gun control, made a mess of the national health program and rushed the passage of a toxic tax legislation which will eventually plunge the country into massive economic debt with its accompanying social suffering. May you realize the outcomes of your toxic body burdens.

Here are the key 25-people responsible for the 2008 Economic Disaster. None of whom were held accountable:

- Alan Greenspan, chairman US Federal Reserve 1987-2006
- Mervyn King, governor of the Bank of England
- Bill Clinton, former US president
- Gordon Brown, former prime minister
- George W. Bush, former US president
- Adam Applegarth, former Northern Rock boss
- Senator Phil Gramm
- Ralph Cioffi and Matthew Tannin
- Joseph Cassano, AIG financial products
- Angelo Mozilo, Countrywide Financial
- Jimmy Cayne, former Bear Sterns boss
- Geir Haarde, prime minister of Iceland 2006-2009
- John Tiner, FSA chief executive 2003-07
- Maurice "Hank" Greenberg, former chief executive AIG insurance group
- Andy Hornby, former HBOS boss
- Fred Goodwin, former RBS boss
- Dick Fuld, chief executive, Lehman Brothers
- Steve Crawshaw, former B&B boss
- Lewis 'Lew' Ranieri, 'godfather' of mortgage finance
- Chuck Prince, former Citi boss
- Stan O'Neal, former boss of Merrill Lynch

- Christopher Dodd, former chairman Senate banking committee, and
- The American Public, for their selfish greed and stupidity
  Plus, two honorary 'toxic' females
- Abby Cohen, Goldman Sachs senior strategist, and
- Kathleen Corbet, former CEO Standard & Poor's.

A couple of males responsible for the opioid epidemic.

Michael Friedman and Howard Udell, Purdue Pharma executives. They argued that they bore no responsibility for the outbreak of "hillbilly heroin" addiction in the U.S. They were convicted in a $634 million settlement that ended the investigation into the company's marketing of OxyContin. These toxic mutant males are now suing to overturn the Health and Human Services department's decision to bar them from working with companies that do business with the federal government. In the 1990s and early 2000s Purdue Pharma used grants, subsidies and artful fakery to spread the notion among leading medical organizations that opioids, especially its new narcotic, OxyContin, weren't addictive for chronic pain patients. Profits over people!

The wealthiest 1% of the world's population now owns more than half of the world's wealth, according to a Credit Suisse report. Since mutant males are all about greed and the need to feed their male vanity, they get on a list:

- Larry Ellison (U.S.) Co-founder, Oracle.
- Carlos Slim Helu (Mexico) Chairman, América Móvil.
- Mark Zuckerberg (U.S.) Co-founder and CEO, Facebook

- Amancio Ortega (Spain) Co-founder, Zara.
- Jeff Bezos (U.S.) CEO, Amazon
- Warren Buffett (U.S.) CEO, Berkshire Hathaway.
- Bill Gates (U.S.) Co-founder, Microsoft.
- Sam Walton and James "Bud" Walton, Walmart
- The Koch Brothers, Koch Industries
- The Mars Family, Mars, Inc.
- The Rothschild Family, Banking

And last, but of course not least, testosterone toxic mutant male "Leaders":

- **Bashar al-Assad, President of Syria**
- Rodrigo Duterte, President of the Philippines
- King Mswati III, Swaziland
- Hu Jintao, China
- King Abdullah bin Abdul-Aziz, Saudi Arabia
- Teodoro Obiang Nguema Mbasogo, Equatorial Guinea
- Islam Karimov, Uzbekistan
- Muammar al-Gaddafi, Libya
- Than Shwe, Burma
- Robert Mugabe, Zimbabwe
- Omar al-Bashir, Sudan
- Kim Jong-Il, North Korea
- Vladimir Putin, the Russian Federation
- Donald Trump, United States of America

33.   SUMMARY

You may not agree with some (or all) of this book, yet the information presented is available on the web and in many other books. There you can find greater detailed scientific explanations than what I have explained here. What I am trying to show is how our every action has consequences. Whether negative or positive depends upon you. The heavy metals in your drinking water is why your child has trouble with math. The plastic bag you threw away strangled a sea turtle. The fungicide you sprayed on your roses is why your mother has cancer. Investing in a company whose focus is on renewable energy may prevent further desecration of wilderness areas from fracking which saves your drinking water. Electing ethical, intelligent, compassionate people with vision and getting rid of corrupt politicians, may help secure your children's futures and your old age.

Our species behaves badly towards itself, other species and the planet. The source of this behavior is partly due to our nature, but this nature can evolve into something better. Teachers have emerged within every generation. They have tried to guide our development as human beings. Their lesson is simple; have respect for life. But it seems the influences of short-sighted, self-indulgent, profit-motivated (toxic, mutant) males stagnates us. Their behavior and attitudes manipulate our thinking and promotes the fears we have about others, the greed we feed with stuff, and the disrespect we have towards life. It is always easier to sink than it is to swim.

My hope is that for some, this information will inspire you to join in cooperative efforts towards correcting the damaging legacy that mutant male thinking has created. If you are not interested in taking action, because you are not a joiner, then perhaps it will inspire you to evaluate your own thinking and behavior towards others. Baby steps.

Eventually, I hope more of you evaluate your behavior towards the Earth you live on and take for granted. We can no longer behave like primitives with cell phones, Facebook accounts and access to nuclear weapons. We need to recover the 14 IQ points we lost.

If nothing else, please stop tolerating toxic mutant behavior and speak out when you encounter it. Do not continue to enable it in the world. Hold those who lie, cheat and steal accountable for their actions. Whether they are executives of giant multinational corporations, supposed leaders of a country, (who *seem* to have all the power and money) or a person in a checkout line insulting the clerk. *Remember, you give to others the power they have over you.*

This is a pivotal time for human life and all life on this planet. We can continue with bigotry, prejudice, hatred and repression of ourselves for our differences, whether gender or race. We can continue destroying the biosphere that supports us. We can wipe ourselves out with "weapons of mass destruction". (The fact that we even have weapons of mass destruction alerts you to the path we seem to be taking.) Whatever way we decide to wipe ourselves out, the Earth will continue to exist without us. Remember, it has already witnessed at least six mass extinctions. What type of humans we want to be and what type of future we want to live in (or die in), is up to all of us. The choice is ours.

I did not do footnotes or references because you have open access to all this information through the internet. If you doubt some of the science or need references, just "Google". Besides, does the Twitter generation really read footnotes? I think not. Anyway, I hope this information gets you thinking.   Because it isn't about what is happening to somebody else, this is about what is happening to you.

www.ingramcontent.com/pod-product-compliance
Lightning Source LLC
Chambersburg PA
CBHW051912250726
48659CB00002B/604